Rev. V

The Nail of Jahel

Lives of the Old Testament Heroines for Catholic Girls

St. Jerome Library
Metamora, Indiana
Copyright ©2017, 2021 St. Jerome Library Press
www.stjeromelibrary.org

Dedicated to all the Catholic girls of our St. Gertrude the Great School

Contents:

Foreword

This book started in the summer of 2015, when the parish where I work hosted one of our annual summer camps for girls. St. Gertrude the Great Roman Catholic Church, which is located in West Chester, Ohio, organizes summer camps for girls and boys every year. The children, many of whom are students in our St. Gert-rude the Great School, get a chance there to spend a few days in play, prayer, sports, and arts. Our little church, founded in 1978 by Bishop Daniel L. Dolan, is a Traditional Catholic parish and all our priests celebrate the Holy Sacrifice of the Mass according to the Missal of Pope St. Pius X.

During the three-day camp I preached to the girls about some of the Old Testament heroines, Rahab, Jahel, and Judith. In the sermons I wanted to tell the children how the Catholic girls of our age, the future mothers of a Catholic family, can and should learn a lot from the Saints of the Old Law. After the camp I gave more sermons about other heroines, like Eve and Agar, in our St. Hugh of Lincoln Church in Milwaukee, Wisconsin. The sermons eventually grew into a collection of biographies of other heroines as well, starting from Eve all the way to the Machabees.

When the young Catholics of our times grow up a bit, they will encounter many accusations against the Biblical heroes and heroines, and, what is worse, against God and His Church. With this book I wish to help them to know their Catholic Faith better, and to grow in admiration of the past generations of God's servants on Earth. And the more they know and learn to love these past generations, who sacrificed so much for

God's service, the more they can also pass on this love to the new generations of Catholics. In the modern age of the world – the true Dark Ages – the only answer to the problems of mankind and of society as a whole is humility in God's service, and faithful and humble obedience to the commandments of His Church, under the protection of the Blessed Virgin Mary.

Fr. Vili Lehtoranta

West Chester, OH
February 3, 2016
on the feast of St. Blaise BM
within the Octave of St. Francis de Sales

Foreword to the second edition:

This revised edition of *The Nail of Jahel* has been published by St. Jerome Library Press. I am very grateful to Mrs. Nicole McGinnis and a Catholic friend of hers for the work they have done in proofreading the text and leaving feedback.

Chapter 1

Eve

The woman therefore saw that the tree was good
to eat, and fair to the eyes, and delectable to behold:
and she took of the fruit thereof, and did eat.

- Genesis 3:6

The Old Testament contains many examples of great women confessors of the Faith, called heroines. And the first one of them was the very first woman ever created, that is, *Eve*. If there ever was a woman who was in desperate need of salvation, she was our mother according to the flesh, Eve, the wife of Adam, the first man. She is truly the greatest and most sinful woman who ever lived. But she, our first mother, was also redeemed by her own descendant, Jesus.

After God created the first man, He created Eve for him as a helper like himself.[1] She was given to Adam as a wife, and so it was from the very beginning of the creation of man, when God established marriage. It was God in His goodness Who provided a help for the man that there might not be anything under man's care that was not good. God also knew full well what a blessing the gender of Mary would be to him, and also to the Church.[2]

Adam and Eve were destined to remain in the Garden of Eden for a while and then obtain eternal happiness. But the Heavenly Father desired the free service of mankind, not the servitude of slaves. Therefore God placed Adam and Eve on trial, as He had placed the angels before them. He did this so that Adam and Eve and their progeny might acknowledge His almighty power, and also so that they might merit everlasting happiness.

The trial of Adam and Eve consisted in a command given by God, which forbade them to eat the fruit of a tree. God had planted two special trees in Paradise: the Tree of Life, which stood in the middle of Paradise, and the tree of knowledge of good and evil.[3] He said to Adam: "But of the tree of knowledge of good and evil eat thou not. For in what day soever thou shalt eat of it, thou shalt die the death."[4] This command demanded an act of submission on the part of Adam and Eve. They were free to say "yes" or "no" as they willed. Their choice would prove whether they loved God or not.

In this test God willed Satan, who in his rebellion had forfeited his own happiness and was jealous of man's happiness, to tempt Eve. Therefore Satan disguised himself under the appearance of a serpent and glided into the Garden. He was resolved, if possible, to make Adam and Eve the companions of his ruin through sin and, in this way, destroy the whole human race in its origin.

But Satan was too cunning to appeal directly to Adam. Instead, Satan tempted him through his wife, saying to Eve: "No, you shall not die the death. For God doth know that in what day soever you shall eat thereof, your eyes shall be opened: and you shall be as Gods, knowing good and evil."[5] Satan tempted Eve by pride, that fountainhead of all sin, and Eve failed in the trial of obedience, and willfully violated God's command. Eve played with temptation by listening to the serpent and by entering into conversation with him. She yielded to curiosity by inspecting the forbidden fruit instead of turning away. She believed the lie of Satan rather than the warning of God, and yielding to pride, broke God's command. And after giving way to pride, she took and ate the fruit. In this way, the first sin on earth was com-mitted.

In all these ways Eve became the occasion of sin to Adam. He was too clear-sighted and strong to be tempted directly, but he was caught in the snare of human respect. Adam loved his

wife and rather than offend her by refusing her pressing invitation to taste of the fruit, he chose to offend God instead. By yielding, Adam showed that he placed the wish of Eve above the command of his Creator.

The seriousness of an offense is measured not only by the nature of the sin, but also by the dignity of the person offended. Eve choose deliberately to offend the infinite Creator of the universe. And her sin was grave. Indeed, the sin of Adam and Eve, after the sin of the angels, was greater than any other.

The guilt of Eve's sin was magnified by the fact that, having received sanctifying grace, she offended the loving Heavenly Father, who had adopted her by grace as His daughter and had given her a wholly undeserved and un-merited right to eternal happiness.

Even before her fall, Eve saw the seriousness of breaking God's command. She was not tempted to eat the fruit because of hunger, as there were plenty of other fruit trees in the garden. And her passions or natural inclinations did not lead her on, because her intellect was strong, clear and unclouded, and her bodily tendencies were under the firm control of her will. Therefore, the sacrifice which was asked of her was small and easy to make. But despite the easiness of the command, and despite the clearness of her knowledge, Eve gave full and free consent to the act of disobedience. Her sin was an act of shameful ingratitude toward God, who had showered her and her husband with gifts. By her sin, Eve showed that she despised the promise of everlasting happiness with God.

After the fall God questioned Adam. But

the first man dodged his guilt by saying: "The woman which thou gavest me to be my fellow-companion, gave me of the tree, and I did eat."[6] Notice: the woman that *you* gave me, as if to say, "this disaster *you* placed on my head." Adam was a coward. He had no humility to accuse himself, and no scruples to accuse God instead. Then God came to Eve and said to her: "Why hast thou done this?"[7] as if He was saying: "If you would only say: 'Forgive me,' to humble your soul and be forgiven." But again, just like with Adam, Eve stayed un-repentant. No pleas of forgiveness. She only answered: "The serpent deceived me, and I did eat," as if to say: "If the serpent did wrong, what concern is that to me?" While Adam and Eve should have knelt in repentance and acknowledged their deepest fault and shame, neither one stooped to self-accusation. No trace of humility was found in them.[8]

Because of her unrepentance, God said to Eve: "I will multiply thy travails and thy child-bearings: in travail shalt thou bring forth children, and thou shalt be under thy husband's power, and he shall have dominion over thee."[9]

This sentence of punishment, which God pronounced on Eve, did not apply only to her, but also to all women after her. Woman was subject to man even before the fall, as wife must always be to her husband. But before the fall this subjection only implied good order, not any hard-ship or abuse on the part of man. It was different, now that Adam and Eve had sinned. Subjection became servitude and liable to all sorts of abuses.

After the interrogation, and finding them unrepentant, God put His punishment into action. God made for Adam and Eve garments of skins and clothed them, and then He said: "Adam is become as it were one of us, knowing good and evil: now therefore, lest perhaps he reach forth his hand, and take also of the tree of life, and eat, and live for ever." Then God cast Adam and Eve out of Paradise to work the earth of which he was taken. And He placed Cherubims and a flaming sword to guard the tree of life.[10] The angels were put there to prevent Adam and Eve from attempting to return to fetch of the fruit of the tree of life. If they had tried to eat this means of immortality in a state of sin, it could only have brought them ever-lasting damnation.

In the banishment of Adam and Eve we see clearly and beautifully both the mercy and the justice of God in action. He had threatened Adam and Eve with death, if they ate of the forbidden fruit, and what He threatened was now fulfilled. But in His mercy, almighty God did not make our first parents die immediately, for they were not hardened in sin, and were capable of amendment. But from that moment on their bodies lost the supernatural gift of immortality,

and their souls lost that grace which was their life. Eve was now truly worse than dead: she had "died the death", that is, she was now in the state of mortal sin.

The lowliness and shame into which Eve had sunk is well described in a poem of John Whitaker Watson named *Beautiful Snow*:

Once I was pure as the snow – but I fell:
Fell, like the snow-flakes, from heaven – to hell:
Fell, to be tramped as the filth of the street:
Fell, to be scoffed, to be spit on and beat.
       Pleading,
          Cursing,
               Dreading to die,
Selling my soul to whoever would buy,
Dealing in shame for a morsel of bread,
Hating the living and fearing the dead.
Merciful God! have I fallen so low?
And yet I was once like this beautiful snow!

Once I was fair as the beautiful snow,
With an eye like its crystals, a heart like its glow;
Once I was loved for my innocent grace –
Flattered and sought for the charm of my face.
      Father,
           Mother,
                  Sisters all,
God, and myself, I have lost by my fall.
The veriest wretch that goes shivering by
Will take a wide sweep, lest I wander too nigh;
For of all that is on or about me, I know
There is nothing that's pure but the beautiful
snow.[11]

The evil consequences of original sin corrupted the whole human race, and all men are by birth "children of wrath."[12] We are all subject to suffering and death, and nobody could attain heaven, if our divine Redeemer had not been born into this world to be given as a sacrifice for our sins. Adam and Eve, having sinned through their pride and disobedience, were humbled by the degrading sentence: "Dust thou art, and into dust thou shalt return."[13] On Ash Wednesday the Church reminds us in a special manner by placing the ashes on our foreheads that we are but dust and ashes, and that we shall surely die: "Remember, man, that thou art dust, and into dust thou shalt return."

The fall was the beginning of the sad history of the human race. After having had the joy of becoming a mother of two sons, Eve had the immense grief to see her dear son, Abel, murdered by her other son, Cain. Cain began by being envious of his brother, and then, because he, just like his parents, did not check his mutiny, there grew in his heart a fierce anger against Abel. God Himself warned Cain, as He had warned his parents: "The lust thereof shall be under thee."[14] But Cain gave in to anger, which then turned into bitter hatred, until at last it led

18

him to commit the terrible crime of the first murder. And just like his mother, Cain refused to beg forgiveness, and instead answered God, when asked where his brother was: "I know not, am I my brother's keeper?"[15] And just like his parents, Cain was driven away from the Face of God and became a fugitive.[16] And his poor mother, Eve, had to then weep over the body of her beloved son, Abel, slain by the hand of his brother. She wept not only for the loss of Abel, but also for the crime and banishment of Cain, as well as for her own pride and disobedience, which was the cause of her own suffering, the suffering of her husband, and the suffering of her sons.

There is an ancient legend, that the Archangels Michael and Uriel buried Adam and Abel in the regions of Paradise. Eve saw this with her son Seth, but nobody else saw this last glimpse of Paradise on earth. Six days after Adam's death, Eve knew that her own death was approaching, so she gathered together all her sons and daughters. She warned them that because of the fall of her and Adam, God would pour the wrath of His judgment upon the human

race,
the first
time by
water,
and the
second
time by
fire.
And
after
she had
finis-
hed her
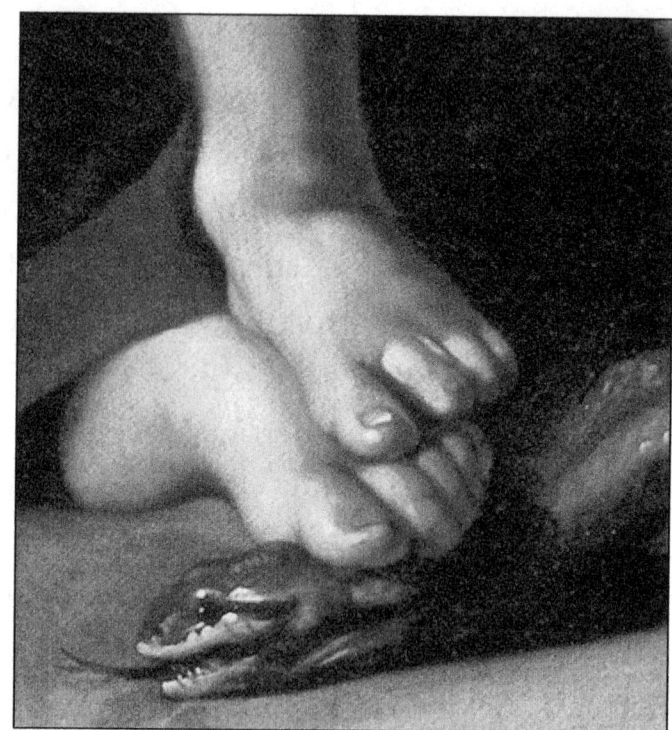
talk, Eve stretched out her hand toward heaven, knelt upon the earth, worshipped God, and giving thanks, died. Afterwards all her children buried her with great weeping.[17]

But before all this took place, before the sad start of the history of the fallen human race, and before Almighty God drove Adam and Eve out of Paradise into the misery of the outside world, He gave them the promise of a Redeemer. The thought that by their sin they had condemned themselves and their children to misery in this world and eternal ruin in the next,

would have driven Adam and Eve into despair. But God awakened in their hearts the hope of a coming Savior. The curse pronounced on the infernal serpent contained a consolation for fallen man. God told the devil: "I will put enmities between thee and the woman, and thy seed and the seed of her: she shall bruise thy head in pieces, and thou shalt lie in wait of her heel."[18]

In these words God told Adam and Eve that sin and the devil would be overcome some day, and the gates of the heavenly Paradise would be thrown open to them. If even our first parents, who committed the most grievous sin which was ever possible to make, were finally saved by the birth and death of one man, our Lord Jesus Christ, how could any one of us doubt that in the end God will in His mercy save us as well? The birth of Jesus has given every Catholic, young and old, a reason for lifelong rejoicing. The Catholic religion is – despite all the efforts to prove the opposite – a religion of happiness. That a young Catholic knows the true hope and meaning of his life, makes him happy even in the midst of sorrows. And this hope is well described in the words taken from the Divine Office of Christmas Eve, the feast fittingly containing the name of our first mother: "Sanctify yourselves, O ye children of Israel, saith the Lord: for on the morrow the Lord will come down. And will take away from you all sickness. On the morrow the sins of the earth shall be washed away, and the Saviour of the world will be our King."[19]

Chapter 2

Agar

And an angel of God called Agar from heaven,
saying: What doest thou Agar? fear not: for
God hath heard the voice of the boy.

- Genesis 21:17

Next I want to take you to the time of the patriarchs and prophets, and tell you about a mother named *Agar*. She was the wife of Abraham and mother of his son Ismael. Abraham lived originally in the city named Haran, together with his wife Sarai and his nephew, Lot. But God commanded him to leave the country of his fathers and go to a new country He would show him, the Promised Land, the Land of Chanaan.[20]

Chanaan was the place which God Himself had prepared for Abraham and his family, and the place where Jesus would one day be born.

In an old Finnish hymn named *O Land of Chanaan*, the Promised Land is compared to Heaven, which is the home of God and also the real home of every Christian:

My beautiful home in Heaven, I got it together with Jesus. / I no longer desire the world, in which I formerly got my joy. / There the Lamb of God shines, even brighter than the sun. / And the marvellous crown of victory is given to us. / O Land of Chanaan, o beautiful land, the Land where Jesus is. / There the Children of God will stay and live forever. / Give thanks to our Lord.

Even though Abraham was the natural father of many nations – that's what his name signifies – he was the spiritual father of many more, that is, of all those who are members of the Catholic Church until the end of the world, some of whom are Jews, the descendants of Sarai, but the greatest part Gentiles, including the children of Ismael.

Since Abraham could not have children with Sarai, she gave to him her Egyptian hand-maid named Agar as wife. But after Agar was with child, she started to despise Sarai. And when

Agar was corrected for her bad behavior, she ran away. In her distress, she fled far away from home, and the angel of God found her, and asked her: "Agar, the handmaid of Sarai, whence comest thou? and whither goest thou?" And she answered: "From the face of Sarai my mistress do I fly." The angel told her to return home to Abraham and humble herself under Sarai, giving her to understand that the fault was wholly on her side.[21]

The angel then told Agar: "Multiplying will I multiply thy seed, and it shall not be numbered for the multitude thereof. Behold, thou art with child, and thou shalt bring forth a son; and thou shalt call his name Ismael, because the Lord hath heard thine affliction."[22]

Until now Agar had imagined that she was talking to some man. But now she realized that it was an angel of God, and she cried towards God calling Him: "Thou the God which hast seen me." The ancients generally believed that death would strike someone who has seen God or His angel, and therefore she added: "Verily here have I seen the back parts of him that hath seeth me." Having now obtained pardon from God, she

she returned home and gave birth to a son who was named Ismael, as the angel had said. Ismael's birth was a remarkable event, since it had been foretold by an angel, an honor shown to very few, like Isaac, Solomon and St. John the Baptist.[23]

Abraham now had a son, of whom many nations would spring. But Ismael was not meant to be the one who would possess the Promised

Land and promised Messiah. After the birth of Ismael, God said to Abraham:

> And I will make thee increase exceedingly, and I will make thee into Nations, and Kings shall come forth of thee. And I will establish my covenant between me and thee, and between thy seed after thee in their generations by a perpetual covenant: to be thy God, and thy seeds after thee. And I will give to thee, and to thy seed the land of thy peregrination, all the land of Chanaan for a perpetual possession, and I will be their God.[24]

Then the time came for Isaac to be born, and it was from this child that Jesus was to be born one day. On the day of the great feast that Abraham prepared, when he circumcised and weaned Isaac, Sarai noticed Ismael playing with him.

She saw, now when Ismael was older, how much he shared the characteristics of his mother. Just as Sarai had been despised in the eyes of Agar, so too Ismael was now mocking Isaac. Sarai therefore thought, that if Ismael acts in this way towards her son while she is still alive, perhaps Abraham will make Ismael the coheir with her son Isaac when she dies.[25]

For this reason, Sarai said to Abraham: "Cast out this handmaid and her son." Abraham was very sad, but God promised him that He would protect Agar and Ismael, saying: "The son also of the handmaid I will make into a great nation, because he is thy seed."[26]

So Abraham rose up in the morning, took some bread and a bottle of water, and sent Agar and Ismael away. He meant to send them only to the neighborhood, where he would take care to provide for her and Ismael. But Agar lost her way and wandered to the wilderness of Bersabee. When the water run out, she cast the boy under a tree, and wept. But God heard the affliction of Ismael, and again an angel talked to Agar saying: "What doest thou Agar? fear not; for God hath heard the voice of the boy, from the place wherein he is. Arise, take up the boy, and hold his hand; for into a great nation will I make him."[27]

And God opened her eyes. Agar saw a well, and went and filled the bottle, and gave Ismael to drink. And as He had promised, God made a great nation out of him. Agar took a wife for him from her native land Egypt, and he lived in the wilderness of Pharan.[28]

In her distress, Agar raised her voice towards the Heavenly Father. And God opened the eyes of Agar. Nothing was of any help to her before the visit of an angel. God wanted to give evidence of care on His part. He made clear to Agar how ignorant she was, and showed her the way to find the place flowing with springs of water. When she was in need, God answered her. When she had lost all hope of survival, God gave evidence of His generosity by consoling her and at the same time taking care of her child. In a similar way, whenever God wishes, if we are all alone and abandoned, if we are in desperate trouble, or even if we have no hope of survival, we need no other assistance. God's grace is all we require. If we win favor from Him, we will be victorious against anyone. The grace of God is the greatest security in life and the strongest

possible fortification.[29]

But how often we have shown ourselves to be like spoiled little children as Ismael was, seeking not only to do our own will instead of that of our Father, but also to lure the family and friends of ours to do alike. It is *sin* which casts us away from our Father's house, out into the wilderness, and then we are at the mercy of our Mother, the Blessed Virgin Mary. She pleads to the Father, that we would not die in our thirst of mercy. We have her promise that she will hear and pray for us, so that we also will become part of God's great nation, as His adopted children.

It is for this reason that the devil goes so hard after those sinners who, although having lost the divine grace by mortal sin, still cherish some devotion to the Blessed Virgin Mary. Sarai, seeing Isaac playing with Ismael, who was teaching him evil habits, asked Abraham to send him away, as well as his mother Agar also: "Cast out this handmaid and her son." Sarai was not satisfied that the son alone should leave the house without the mother, fearing that later on Ismael would come to visit his mother, and thus continue to frequent the house. In a similar way, the devil is not satisfied with seeing Jesus cast out from a soul, if he does not see the mother also cast out. The devil fears that the mother, by her intercession, may again obtain the return of Jesus. And he has cause to fear, for anyone who is faithful in honoring the mother of God, will eventually also receive her Son. It is for this reason that Our Lady is specially addressed as "the protectress of the condemned."[30]

Agar referred to Almighty God as "the God which hast seen me." Of all the nations and all the peoples on earth, every baptized Catholic has been seen by God, and picked up by His hand-maid, Mary. As Agar without water, a Catholic girl will gain nothing, if she trusts the world, except being banished to a lifeless wilderness.

But she is not a banished orphan anymore, but has been recommended to Mary, who guides her through the wilderness to Heaven, the Land of Chanaan. Of this land the Catholics remaining on Earth are the future inhabitants, as God said: "The son also of the handmaid I will make into a great nation."

Chapter 3

Rahab

𝔑ow therefore swear to me by the 𝔏ord, that as 𝔍 have done mercy with you, so you also do with my father's house. 𝔖he therefore did let them down by a cord out of a window: for her house joined fast to the wall.

- Josue 2:12,15

In the Land of Chanaan, before God's chosen people conquered it according to the promise given to Abraham, there lived another Old Testament heroine named *Rahab*. She was saved by the people of God, because she showed mercy and kindness to them under the threat to her own life.

After the death of Moses, the Israelites were about to enter the Promised Land, and God gave them Josue as their new leader. Immediately he aroused his army into a spirit of combat. The Israelites were fearless soldiers and were successful in the battle.

But to conquer the land God had promised them, they needed first to capture a city named Jericho. So Josue sent two spies to Jericho. There these two found lodging at the house of a woman named Rahab. But the King of Jericho came to know that two Israelites had come to his city by night and were staying at Rahab's house. Rahab hid them on the top of her house and covered them with stalks of flax. Therefore the King's troops did not find them, and the gates of Jericho were closed, so that they could not escape.[31]

Rahab went to the Israeli spies she was hiding and told them she believed this land was given to them by the true God. She only asked that as she showed mercy to them, by hiding them from the soldiers, the Israelites would show mercy to her and to her family. She asked them to save her parents, siblings, and house,

when they would come to conquer Jericho.[32]

The spies promised that Rahab and her family would be shown mercy for protecting them. Then Rahab let them down with a cord out of her window, for her house was next to the wall. The spies said that when the Israelites would come to conquer Jericho, Rahab should tie this purple cord, and collect all her family into her house. The cord would be the sign to the Israelites that this is Rahab's house, she who protected them, and that all its inhabitants must be saved.[33]

Jericho was now closed shut and fenced, because of the fear of the Israelites. According to the commandment of God, Josue had the priests sound seven trumpets, while walking around the city with the ark of the covenant. And on the seventh day, Josue ordered the Israelites to attack the city, but to spare Rahab and her family. All the Israelites shouted with the trumpets, and the walls of Jericho fell down.[34]

In Rahab we see how God saves and rewards all those who stay faithful and do according to His commandments. St. James in his Catholic Epistle in the New Testament says: "Do you see that by works a man is justified: and not by faith only? And in like manner also Rahab the harlot, was not she justified by works, receiving the messengers, and putting them forth another way?"[35] Rahab was not a member of the chosen people, and likewise all of us, every single one who is born into this world, is an alien to God's mercy, because of original sin. Rahab and her family were doomed to perish in the siege of Jericho. But she confessed the true faith, saying to spies: "For the Lord your God He is God in heaven above, and in the earth beneath."[36]

And endangering her own life, that the two strangers, the servants of the living God, might escape unharmed, Rahab helped them escape. Be-

cause she showed and did mercy, she was also shown mercy by God. Not only was she saved from the destruction of Jericho, but she and her family were taken as members of the chosen people, and she married Salmon, of the tribe of Juda. Salmon and Rahab were the parents of Booz[37] and in this way, a foreign woman of Chanaan became the ancestor of King David, and also of Our Lord Jesus.

This heroine of the Old Law did in her life prove to the later generations, that God's servants can sweeten even the darkest and most

sorrowful corners of the earth. One fifth century Syrian Bishop had these beautiful words to say in praise of Rahab: "In the midst of the land of impiety there was a pearl, in the mire there was burnished gold, in the mud there was a flower blooming with godliness."[38] It is remarkable, how often the centuries have described Rahab as a beautiful flower. This introducing a pagan girl into the Jewish nation was a truly extraordinary event. Jews are very exclusive and cautious against strangers in their midst, but Rahab's heroism in saving the Israeli spies was something truly memorable. It's true, the seed where she grew came from an impious soil, but God Who showed mercy, accepted her, planted, and raised her among His other beautiful flowers. Rahab, just like Ruth, who later married her son Booz, was made an ancestor of Jesus, because she believed in God, and showed mercy to His servants.

Even Jews themselves, after the centuries passed, and when they had committed many horrible crimes, and even rejected our Lord on the Cross, still did not forget this pagan girl, who became the ancestor of King David through her heroism. They have a religious book called the Talmud, which they still study, and where one can find this passage:

What does the king do? He makes his son a garden: as long as the son obeys his father's injunctions, the latter visits all the universe to find the most beautiful flowers and have them transplanted into the son's garden. But, if he is vexed by his son's behaviour, he pulls up all the flowers. It is the same thing for the Israelites when they do God's will. He goes over all the world and seeks amongst the other nations for a wise man, and he brings him to the Israelites and unites him to their nation, as, for instance, Jethro and Rahab. But when they vex the Lord, he takes from them even the just men who are among them.[39]

Rahab loved her father, her mother, and her brothers and sisters so much, that she willingly risked her life that her whole family might be taken into the sweet communion of God's saints. Like Rahab, every Catholic was once a little baby, born without grace, and living far away from God, excluded from the company of saints. But his parents brought him to a priest, that he might baptize him, wash away his sins, and make him a true child of Almighty God. Without the faith and heroic deeds of their daughter Rahab, her father and mother would have perished in the destruction of Jericho, together with her brothers and sisters. And if the parents of a Catholic child had not brought him to be baptized, the priest could not have washed his sins away, and made him a child of God and a member of Christ's Mystical Body on Earth, the church of the Saints, the Catholic Church. A true child of God never

returns this gift of Baptism with ingratitude, disobedience, or unfaithfulness, but in all his actions shows, that God has made him His good and faithful servant, as He once made the foreign girl of Chanaan, Rahab.

Chapter 4

Jahel

𝕭lesseb among women be Jahel and blesseb be she in her tabernacle. 𝕳er left hand she put to the nail, and her right hand to the smith's hammer, and struck 𝕾isara.

𝕭etween her feet he fell, and bied. 𝕳e was rolled between her feet, and he lay without life and miserable.

- Judges 5:24, 26-27

The woman named *Jahel* is greatly praised in the Old Testament as a heroine, who fearlessly defeated the enemy of God's chosen people. Jahel saved the northern nation of Israel, but she herself, like Rahab, was not one of the chosen people of God. She belonged to a tribe called Kenites, who were coppersmiths and metal-workers. They did not mingle with the Israelites, but lived in the Promised Land, maintaining their distinct, nomadic lifestyle. The Israelites, on the other hand, started to worship idols, so God punished them by sending the King of Chanaan, named Jabin, to war with Israel. The king of the Chananites, whom Josue had driven away from the Promised Land, now came back with a vengeance, and his attack was led by the general named Sisara.[40]

Fearing for the fate of their country, the Israelites asked advice from a judge named Debbora, who was a good and pious woman. She called a man called Barac and told him that God would give victory to Israel, if he would lead the army. But Barac was timid, and did not dare to go, unless Debbora would come with him. So Debbora told him that victory will not be attributed to Barac, but Sisara will be killed by the hand of a woman.[41]

When Sisara saw the troops of Barac, he was frightened, and retreated. Barac's army of Israelites defeated the troops of Chanaan, but Sisara escaped, and sought refuge in the lands of Haber of the Kenite tribe.[42] Haber's family was pious, and lived in recluse on land away from the Israelites, because he was disgusted about the idol worship of the Israelites.

When Sisara arrived, Haber was out, but his wife Jahel came to him, and asked him to come in and rest. Exhausted from fleeing, Sisara asked for some water; Jahel gave him milk, and also a blanket to rest upon.[43]

Jahel was very good at keeping the household. She stayed home and took care of Haber's house when he was out farming or trading in the marketplace. The house really was not a house, but a tent, or a *tabernacle*, as the Douay Bible calls it. The tents of the Kenites were huge. They were places of living, not of camping. A tent could be fifty feet long and twenty feet wide, and the ropes and their nails were very big. The wind would work the tent nails loose, and the people

living in them had to pound them back into the ground over and over.

When Sisara fell asleep from exhaustion, Jahel took one of the nails of her tent, and a hammer. Then sneaking silently to sleeping Sisara, she carefully placed her nail on the temples of Sisara's head, so that he would not awake. And then with one big stroke, she hit the nail with the hammer, piercing it through Sisara's head fast into the ground. And that was the end of Sisara.[44]

When Barac came in pursuit of Sisara, Jahel went out to meet him and said: "Come, and I will show thee the man whom thou seekest." And when Barac came into the tent of Jahel, he

saw Sisara, lying there dead, and the nail of Jahel fastened in his temples. Evil king Jabin was so humiliated that his general was killed by a woman that his own subjects rebel-led and overthrew him.[45]

Did you notice in the story how timid Barac was? God's prophetess Debbora called Barac and told him: "Our Lord God of Israel hath commanded thee: Go, and lead an army - - and I will bring unto thee Sisara and his chariots, and all the multitude, and will deliver them in thy hand."[46] God chose Barac to lead the attack, but he hesitated, so the greatest victory of defeating the enemy was denied him, and his place was given to Jahel.

A girl of a Catholic family should learn to imitate this holy woman Jahel by being humble and obedient at home. She must be faithful not only to the word of the Heavenly Father, but also to her father at home, as Jahel took good care of her husband's tent while he was gone. A girl who acts this way has Our Lady's protection and intercession. She must ask Mary's help to make her a loving daughter of her father and mother.

Unfortunately, most modern girls treat their parents very disrespectfully, as if they were mere air. Recently, while traveling by airplane, I read the *American Way* magazine and there was an editorial written by a father. This man had two daughters, 9-year-old Maddy, and 6-year old Lilly. He wrote that when he recently got home from a long work-related trip, 6-year-old Lilly came all happy and excited to welcome him home with a gleeful shout: "Daddy!" But he took notice, how the older daughter, 9-year old Maddy stayed in the other room, playing *Minecraft* on her iPad. He wrote about how he walked into the room where she was playing and announced his presence, saying:

"Hi, honey! Daddy's home."

"Hey, Dad," she says without looking up.

"I missed you," I say while staring at her, ho-ping she'll take her eyes off the game and come give me a giant hug like she did when she was Lilly's age.

"Missed you, too," she says.

And the game goes on.[47]

Listening to the words and commands of both her Heavenly Father and her father at home is one of the most crucial marks of a Catholic girl. Both the warning of Barac and the sad incident recorded by this neglected father show that it is humility and obedience to the Word of God, and to the word of one's parents, that makes a good Catholic girl. One who neglects to hear these words, hardens his – or in this case her – heart to the true appreciation which a child should show to his or her father.

This same father wrote in the same column how saddened he was that the same rea-son, the desire to work hard and make a good living for his family, was the very reason he was now neglected:

This incident with Maddy was not isolated, al-though it hurt more than most. To be fair, I've been on the road a lot these days. It's hard for me to leave home, much like it was for my dad; much like it's been for every working parent in the history of ever. It's because I've been on the road so much that Lilly was overjoyed when her daddy returned. Yet it's this same frequency of travel that may have hardened Maddy.[48]

This story of Jahel should give a lesson to the Catholic girls, how immensely good is the work the fathers do outside home, and the work mothers do at home. They should see in the story how God can use them in a mighty way, even if they only do their simple things at home, like cleaning, watching their siblings, doing dishes, cooking, or things like that. And even though the parents have big power over their children to command them to do whatever they want them to do, the children also have immense power over their moms and dads. "The confusion of the father is of a son without discipline: and the daughter shall be made of less account. A wise daughter is an inheritance to her husband: for she that confoundeth, is made a contumely to her father."[49] An ungrateful child is a source of great hurt to the father. A Catholic girl never despises neither the work nor the commands of her mom

and dad, because otherwise she earns – or rather, draws down upon her – this biblical title of a foolish daughter.

Also, a Catholic girl needs to show her gratitude for all the hard work her mother does in order to provide a good life for her children. That is the norm of a Catholic family, that the father works outside the home to provide food and shelter for his family, and the mother stays at home, or in Jahel's case, in tent, to look after the things father provides. The equality-loving world claims that women can do things just as well as men can. And in many cases this is true. Women who train to be breadwinners can end up to be very good breadwinners. But they do not necessarily end up very good bread*makers* – or home-makers. The

Catholic girls, the future mothers, should not groom themselves to be an "independent woman" or to make a name or career for themselves. They have the immense power to impact this world's generations by becoming not just mothers, but being women of a Catholic home.[50]

Jahel is a great example to a Catholic girl. She used strength and the things she had on hand. She used the food in her kitchen. She used the tools she had: her hammer and her tent nail. And how mightily did God use her! Jahel was not cruel. She waited until her enemy had fallen asleep with exhaustion, and only then did she quickly and efficiently end his cruel days. Sisara truly never knew what hit him. And what a blessing Jahel got from God. She had her name put into the Holy Scriptures forever.

A Catholic girl does not have to go out to work somewhere outside the home to do the work of God. Even when she still stays at the home of her parents, she can already start doing the work of God by making her mom and dad and their guests comfortable at home. She always

helps her mother in her plans to make the home comfortable, and does not try to play the star of the household, as if everything and everyone should center around herself. Jahel did her household duties with care. If she had not had her star moment with Sisara, sent by God, we would know nothing about her. She, like the Blessed Virgin Mary, was quiet, and went unnoticed by the world, but because of her fidelity, God made her name glorious and raised her into sainthood.

And that's how Catholic girls should seek sanctity as well, in humility and obedience to their parents. I was once discussing the children of one of our mission families with one of our priests. The other priest mentioned one girl of that family, whom he said he really knew nothing about, because she is always so quiet, and it was hard for him to tell what kind of a character she had. I know this girl whom my priestly colleague was talking about. And I said that this is true: she is very quiet, sticks to her role, helps in the home, minds her own business, and stays away from adults' way – which means she is exactly as a well-mannered, good Catholic girl should be.

You see, fathers, mothers, and priests do see the quiet girls in our missions and in our churches, and they appreciate the work of the children at home and at school, even if they don't always express that in words. If a good Catholic girl acts quietly and humbly doing her duty, she should not be depressed if she never gets a word of thanks for her effort. It most likely means that she does an excellent job. We adults are funny creatures in a way, that usually we always find time to offer reproaches for the bad behavior of children, but most of the time stay silent when they act well. I hope the children will forgive us for this fault of ours. It does not mean we don't care, or take no notice of the children, but the fathers, mothers, teachers, and priests know their children well, and we *do* appreciate the good work they do. But even if we adults will occasionally miss all the help the children offer for us at home and at school, the Catholic girls can rest assured, that not a single good deed of theirs goes unnoticed by their Heavenly Father. The story of Jahel tells the girls to love their everyday, humble duties, which might not be a road to world fame or riches, but are a sure way to the riches of Heaven.

Chapter 5
Jephte's Daughter

And she said to her father: This only grant me which I desire: Suffer me that two months I may go about the mountains, and bewail my virginity with my fellows.
- Judges 11:37

With this heroine, I want to emphasize the heroism of a religious vocation, which parents should often mention and talk about to their children. This heroine, whose name is not recorded in the Holy Scripture, is *the daughter of Jephte*, whom her father offered as a burnt sacrifice to God, and who humbly accepted this tribulation.

Jephte lived in a time when the Israelites started again to worship idols. So God sent a foreign tribe called the Ammonites to conquer Israel, and they held it under oppression for eighteen years. The Israelites, since they were desperate in the battle against the Ammonites, went to see a man named Jephte, who was heading a wild band of outlaws, to recruit him and his troops to fight on their side. They promised that Jephte would be their new leader if he succeeded in banishing the Ammonites. So Jephte made a vow, saying: "If thou wilt deliver the children of Ammon into my hands, whosoever shall first come forth out of the doors of my house, and shall meet me returning with peace from the children of Ammon, him will I offer an holocaust to our Lord."[51]

Jephte had great success, and the Ammonites were beaten. But when he returned to his home, the first person who came to greet him was his daughter, his only child. Jephte rent his garments and said: "Woe is me my daughter, thou hast deceived me, and thyself art deceived: for I have opened my mouth to our Lord, and can do no other thing."[52] After hearing about the vow of her father, she willingly offered herself as the burnt offering. She only asked, that she could go to the mountains for two months to mourn that she had to die without marriage. After two months had passed, she returned, and Jephte sacrificed her. This sacrifice started a yearly custom, where the Israeli women would assemble together, and mourn Jephte's daughter for four days.

The story of Jephte's daughter has troubled Christians and Jews alike for thou-sands of years. Many commentaries have attempted to explain away the striking image of Jephte killing his only precious child and offering her up as a burnt offering. It is also repeatedly pointed out, by the enemies of Christianity, how obedience to this seemingly cruel god overlooks the premeditated murder of the daughter. Some others, like the Jehovah's Witnesses, have tried to explain that Jephte did not really kill his daughter, but meant to devote her exclusively to the service of God. In their view, Jephte was sad, because fulfilling the vow meant losing the company of his beloved only child.[53]

But when we look into this free offering given to almighty God, it is clear that Jephte really did sacrifice his daughter. He said:

"Whosoever shall first come forth out of the doors of my house - - him will I offer an holocaust to our Lord."[54] And after the period of mourning, Jephte's daughter "returned to her father, and he did to her as he had vowed."[55]

But the whole lesson of this passage is not in the rashness of Jephte's vow – after all, human sacrifice was forbidden by God – but in the heroic submission of his daughter. For the sake of obedience and humility to the vow made in honor of God in thanksgiving for the liberation of His people, she gave her own life as a sacrifice.

This story of Jephte's daughter gives us the whole beauty of what a religious vocation is. While everyone who has been baptized is called to live a holy life, in a religious vocation someone willingly gives up the luxuries of life to consecrate himself to God's service.

Of course the sorrows which a just servant of God has to go through are not restricted to religious only. The sorrows are part of the life of every Christian. But those sorrows are truly all light in comparison to the humility of the suffering Christ. And this is something the world

can never understand. A Catholic sees the Great
Sacrifice of not a mere man, but God Himself,
every time he goes to Holy Mass. In the Mass,
the priest puts himself in Christ's place to
assume the garments and takes up the
instruments of the Passion. Calvary is before the
priest. He will go up its steps. When the priest
kisses the altar, he is kissing the Cross, and each
bending down to do it, marks one of Christ's falls

from its glorious weight. The washing of the hands takes the priest back to a scene in Pilate's hall of judgment. The flowing wine is the flowing blood from Christ's wounded head, side and feet. During the Canon, the priest nails his own body to the Cross of Sacrifice. At the breaking of the Host he resolves to break his will to do the Will of God. When he covers the chalice, he buries himself with Christ from the world and all its temptations. And at the Blessing, he arises with Christ to the completion of His triumph in the Resurrection.[56]

When one dedicates his or her life to religion, whether it's serving God as a priest, lay-brother, or religious sister, he, by necessity, is put in the war front against the world, and in this sense, a religious vocation is always a mournful separation from the earthly family. St. Anne was mourning when she had to depart from her beloved Mary. Her grief exceeded even that of Abraham when he was commanded to sacrifice his son Isaac. When Mary was three years old, she was presented in the Temple as a sacrifice of praise and thanksgiving.[57] And also Jephte's daughter was in the state of mourning, for she

would never grow up and have children. But faithful to God, she said to him: "My father, if thou hast opened thy mouth to our Lord, do unto me whatsoever thou hast promised, the revenge and victory of thine enemies being granted to thee."[58]

The humility of a faithful servant of God is something the people of the world can never understand. The enemies of the Church desire the disappearance of religious vocations, especially if they can bring that about with the vanishing of chastity. They are constantly on watch and seeking evidence that religious vocations are a thing of the past, and they gloat over even the appearance of a loss of this precious virtue.

But putting temporal benefits before the service of God can never be part of those who dedicate themselves to the service of their crucified Christ. Our Lord Himself said: "Blessed are they that mourn: for they shall be comforted."[59] Mourning means the sadness of the soul. The reason we mourn is our sadness because of sin. In mourning we mourn both the causes of sin – temptations, frailties and dangers – as well as its consequences – the trials and evils of this life. The soul mourns because it wants to go to God in Heaven. Therefore, a Catholic religious follows the beatitude of mourning by doing penance and following strictly the commandments of God's law, and offering himself as a sacrifice in reparation for his sins and the sins of the world.

Jephte's daughter was one of God's humble souls who was mourning. She asked for

a delay of two months, in order that she might go with her companions to the mountains, to bewail her virginity now given up to death. The weeping of her companions did not move her; their grief did not prevail upon her, nor did their lamentations hold her back. But she returned to her father, and of her own will she urged him on when he was hesitating to sacrifice her. She acted of her own free choice so that what was at first an awful thing, became a pious sacrifice.[60]

Clearly God loves and rewards those sacrifices which a humble soul is ready to go through in the middle of all the injustices of the world, and during his struggles for the truth. So greatly does the just person will to serve God that he is even ready to be killed by the enemies of God, because in this way, God's servant, like God Himself, has returned good for evil. He has returned love instead of hatred. In imitation of Abel, thousands of martyrs have struggled for the truth, to the point of death, and have been sacrificed by savage enemies.[61] Numerous and numberless holy men and women have offered themselves as victims for God, both by sacrificing their own lives, like the daughter of Jephte sacrificed hers, or by serving Him in a spirit of humility, consecrating themselves to-tally to God's service, following the example of the Blessed Virgin Mary.

Parents should never love their children more than they love God, so that they would stop them from answering the call of God in a religious vocation. Lots of parents in the history of the Church have gone through the sorrow of "losing" their child to a religious vocation. St. Philomena, herself born as a single daughter to a long-time childless royal couple, made a vow of virginity at eleven, and rejected marriage to an Emperor. Her parents pleaded with her: "O daughter! Have pity on your parents! Have pity on your country!" But she said that her vow to God would take precedence to everything else, and she was beheaded by the cruel Emperor.[62] The Venerable Ursula Benincasa, a 17th century Italian religious, established the order named Sisters of the Hermitage. These were bound to perpetual abstinence and several fast-days. The life of these Sisters was one of the most absolute separation from the world. On the day of their profession the Sisters were allowed to speak with their nearest relatives for the last time. After that, they would never see them again.[63]

Just like with the religious, Jephte's vow to sacrifice his daughter caused her to withdraw from the world for a while – the world filled with idolatry, violence, and wars. Had she lived in the land of Israel, blinded by its false religion and surrounded by its temptations, there is no knowing what she might have become. It should be remembered that her home was that of a bandit and a robber. Moreover, she received the grace to be told when her end would come, and she retired from the world to meditate on the great truths of Faith and of God. In this sense, every Catholic is always and every day exhorted to remember that one day, in one way or another, he will be held accountable for all of his past actions. As the Holy Scriptures put it: "In all thy works remember thy later ends, and thou wilt not sin forever."[64]

Chapter 6
Ruth

All the people that was in the gate answered, and the ancients: We are witnesses: Our Lord make this woman, which entereth into thy house, as Rachel, and Lia, which builded the house of Israel: that she may be an example of virtue in Ephrata, and may have a famous name in Bethlehem.

- Ruth 4:11

As with Jahel and Jephte's daughter, the history of *Ruth* also took place during the time of Judges, before the people of God had a king. It all started when a fierce famine struck the Promised Land. A man named Elimelech, of the tribe of Juda, who lived in Bethlehem, fled the famine to the land of Moab, which was a pagan country south of Ammon, and took his wife Noemi and his two sons with him.[65]

After Elimelech died, his sons took Moabite pagan girls named Orpha and Ruth as their wives. But after ten years of marriage, both sons died, and Noemi, who had lost her husband and children in a strange country, wanted to return to the Promised Land. But since both Orpha and Ruth were very attached to their mother-in-law, they wanted to follow her. Noemi, however, told them to return to their own mothers and find new husbands; she also imparted her blessing, as a final farewell, in thanks for all good which they had done to her sons and herself.[66]

Crying, Orpha kissed Noemi, and returned to Moab. But Ruth insisted upon staying with Noemi, who then said to her: "Behold thy kins

woman is returned to her people, and to her gods, go with her."[67] This was a decisive moment in the life of Ruth, and in the history of our Redeemer as well. Noemi was saying that Ruth, who was still a pagan, belonged to Moab. If she would want to follow her to the land of her husband, she must abandon not only her own family, but also the false gods of her home country. And so great was the attachment of Ruth to her mother-in-law that she said: "Whither soever thou shalt go, I will go: and where thou shalt abide, I also will abide. Thy people my people, and thy God my God."[68]

When Noemi saw that Ruth had determined to follow her in life and in death, she allowed her to be her companion. So together they travelled to Bethlehem. Ruth had now left her home and friends, both because she loved her mother-in-law, and because of her fidelity to her new faith. She had learned to know the true God, the God of Abraham, Isaac, and Jacob, the ancestors of her husband, and now she wished to live with the people of God in the Promised Land. Ruth was a true heroine, steadfast in faith, and willing to give up everything rather than live with unbelievers and place her soul in danger.

When Noemi and Ruth arrived in Bethlehem, Ruth asked if she could go to work in the fields, and glean the ears of corn, which had been left behind after the reapers, as was the custom among the poor. Noemi gave her permission, and Ruth went to collect corn in the field of Booz, who was the cousin of Elimelech,

and a very rich and powerful man. When Booz came from Bethlehem to inspect his fields, he noticed Ruth collecting ears of corn, and asked his overseer who she was. He answered: "This is that Moabite, which came with Noemi, from the country of Moab." Booz learned that Ruth had been working very hard in the field. Also her affection to Noemi, his relative, pleased Booz very much. So Booz went to Ruth and said that from now on, she could work and live in his household. He admired her fidelity and strength in faith, saying: "And that thou hast left thy parents, and the land wherein thou wast born, and art come to a people, which before thou knewest not. Our Lord render unto thee for thy work, and God grant thou mayest receive a full reward of our Lord the God of Israel, to whom thou art come, and under whose wings thou art fled."[69]

When Ruth returned to Noemi, she was informed that Booz was her relative, and said Ruth should stay with Booz's maids. Noemi also started to plan that Ruth should marry Booz, and instructed her to present herself to him for marriage. He was pleased at her fidelity to her family through marriage, and said to Ruth: "Fear not therefore, but whatsoever thou shalt say to me, I will do to thee. For all the people that dwelleth within the gates of my city, know, that thou art a woman of virtue."[70]

Booz's people were pleased with the marriage, and greeted Ruth as "an example of virtue in Ephrata", and that she "may have a famous name in Bethlehem." Booz married Ruth, and she gave birth to a son. The women of Bethlehem congratulated Noemi for the birth of a boy, saying: "For of thy daughter in law is he born, which will love thee: and much better is she to thee, then if thou hadst seven sons." The boy was named Obed, and he grew up to be the grandfather of King David.[71]

How great was the reward of Noemi. By her living faith and good example, she had converted her daughter-in-law Ruth to the true Faith. And in the midst of mourning her husband and sons, Ruth was her true companion and consoler. Ruth was distinguished for her humility and obedience. She asked Noemi's permission to glean and was not ashamed of her poverty.

All Catholic young women should learn from this humility and modesty of Ruth. They must show as great a love for their own parents as Ruth did for Noemi. For this love the Bible praises Ruth. She was retiring, modest and pure. All of Bethlehem testified to her being a virtuous woman. God rewarded her virtue by giving her a good and wealthy husband, and by making her the great-grandmother of King David and also one of the ancestors of Jesus.

How great are the blessings God grants to the followers of Ruth's example, is well seen in the story of Zélie Guérin (1831-1877). She was a young Catholic woman, who had an irresistible sympathy for human sufferings. She had wanted

to become a Sister of Charity of St. Vin-cent de Paul, but the superioress refused her. She became a lace-maker, and like Ruth had supported her mother-in-law, Zélie supported her poor father by her work. Even in the midst of her work she wrapped herself in contemplation, and God was always with her. She thought carefully on the possibility of serving God more fully by marrying a husband who would also work hard for his salvation, and bringing many children into the world who should be consecrated to God's service. And on one day, on St. Leonard's bridge, she passed Louis Martin, and recognized that this was the companion intended for her by God. There was mutual under-standing and delight, the families met, and the two were married. And her wish was fulfilled: of her five surviving children, all five became nuns, the most famous of whom was St. Thérèse of Lisieux, the Little Flower, canonized in 1925.[72]

The story of Ruth is yet another reminder of God's mercy. Though born in a pagan country, Ruth converted, and by her virtues obtained a share in the blessings of Israel, and was even chosen to be an ancestress of the Redeemer. This was a sign from God, that should pagans believe and be converted, they would also share in the salvation which was to spring from Israel. And it is also the sign for Catholics today, that humility, charity and obedience bring blessings from the Almighty, and sacrifice for others His benevolence.

Chapter 7

Judith

Thou art the glory of Jerusalem, thou the joy of Israel, thou the honour of our people: because thou hast done manfully, and thy heart was strengthened, for that thou had loved chastity.

- Judith 15:10-11

The purpose of the book of Judith is to show how the help of God is always available to His faithful, as long as they continue to pledge themselves to God's service. As Our Lady stood faithful at the foot of the Cross, every Catholic girl is called to stay faithful to the true religion of Jesus, no matter how great the obstacles of life seem. Like St. Joan of Arc, Judith also stood faithful and endangered her own life in order to save the honor of her countrymen and the independence of her own nation.

The times back then were hard to her native land of Juda. The story of Judith happened about the year 690 before Christ's birth, and during that time the people of God were again forgetting their Father and Creator and started to worship idols. So God got very angry at them, and the vast pagan country named Assyria attacked the small nation of Juda. The king of Assyria sent there a mighty man named Holofernes, who was the general-in-chief of the Assyrian army. He arrived to conquer the kingdom of Juda, whose king Manasses was then only a boy.

Holofernes had success in his war efforts.

He conquered all the cities and strongholds of the small country of Juda, and he also treated them with horrible cruelty.

Finally he arrived to siege a city named Bethulia, and cut its water supplies. The water having been cut, the situation seemed hopeless. The citizens of Bethulia were so panicked that the elders of the city decided that if help did not come in five days, they would surrender their city to Holofernes. In the meantime, they did penance for their idolatry. They prayed very hard to God and threw ashes on their heads.[73]

In Bethulia there lived a woman named *Judith*. She was a widow, who was very beautiful and very rich, and lived in her own house. She was then about 36 years of age, and many powerful men wanted to marry her. But she wanted to remain a widow, and spent her days in prayer and fasting. Despite her wealth, she took only one meal a day, in the evening, and wore a hair-cloth, which is a rough garment worn under the other clothes, for the purpose of doing penance.[74]

Judith was deeply touched because of the distress of her people. But when she heard that

the elders were planning to surrender to Holofernes, she went to see them and said:

> What is this word - - to yield the city to the Assyrians, if within five days there come no aid to us? And what are you, that tempt our Lord? - - You have set a time for the mercy of our Lord, and according to your pleasure, you have appointed Him a day. But because our Lord is patient, let us be penitent for this same thing, and shedding tears let us desire His pardon: for not as man, so will God threaten, neither as the son of man will he be inflamed to anger. - - And therefore let us not revenge ourselves for these things, which we suffer, but reputing these very punishments to be the

scourges of our Lord, - - let us think them to have chanced to our amendment, and not to our destruction.[75]

The elders were deeply impressed by the noble words of Judith, and they begged her to pray for the people of Juda. So Judith did so, and retired to seclusion, begging God to spare her people. And while she prayed, God inspired her with a plan what she should do.

Judith put away her hair-cloth, and put on her richest and most beautiful clothes. She put on the finest perfume, braided her hair, and adorned herself with bracelets and rings. She had already been beautiful, but now God even increased her beauty, because all her dressing up did not come from vanity.

After all this decoration, Judith took her maid with her, and left her house to go to the camp of Holofernes. When she arrived, Holofernes thought that she had fled from her own people, wanting to escape the definite destruction. He was also struck by Judith's beauty, and so he allowed her to come and go as she plea-sed. On the fourth day Holofernes gave

a big feast to the officers of his army, celebrating the coming surrender of Bethulia. During the feast Holofernes and his soldiers drank too much wine and passed out.

Judith then saw that now God had offered her the chance for which she had waited. She prayed: "Confirm me O Lord God of Israel, and in this hour have respect to the works of my hands, that as Thou hast promised, Thou mayest advance Jerusalem Thy city: and I may bring to pass that which I believing that it may be done by Thee, have purposed."[76] Judith knew that the Assyrians had already conquered several places, and if the strong fortress of Bethulia fell, the way to Jerusalem and to God's Holy Temple would be open to this cruel general. Judith then snuck quietly to the tent of Holofernes. She took his sword, which hung from a pillar nearby, raised it high, and cut off the head of evil Holofernes.[77]

After that, Judith gave the head to her maid, who had waited outside, and she hid it in her purse. Judith then snuck out of the camp and returned with her maid to Bethulia. There she assembled all the people, who were waiting in dread of the rising day, when they would have to surrender to the evil Assyrians. Judith posted herself in front of them, and then, slowly and solemnly showed them the head of Holofernes. The whole city and the elders bursted into praise for God, and praised Judith, who had done such a courageous deed. Shouting with joy and praising God, the people of Bethulia rushed to the camp of the Assyrians.

When the Assyrian soldiers discovered the

headless body of their once mighty general, they panicked. They fled out to the camp shou-ting that Holofernes had been killed. The panic spread in the camp, and when the people of Bethulia arrived, they merely needed to complete the work of Judith, and take possession of the Assyrian camp. Then all the people, turning to Judith, sang a song of praise to her: "Thou art the glory of Jerusalem, thou the joy of Israel, thou the honour of our people."[78] The feasting of this great victory lasted for three months. Judith became famous and respected throughout the nation. She died at the age of 105 years, and was mourned by all the people.

In the history of Judith, God once again showed great mercy to His people. Judith was truly a heroine, because by living a simple and God-fearing life, she was chosen to be her people's liberator.

I want to point out to Catholic girls especially her virtue in Mary-like modesty. They should learn from Judith how to dress properly in the service of God, and how to fight against sin and evil.

Our world is a very sin-filled world. It's of course nothing new that people are sinning. People have been sinning since the Fall. But it is rather the people's *response* to the sin which is the great problem of our age. Modern people have this funny idea, that men have liberty to do whatever they want, even if it goes against the commandments of God. Catholic girls are followers of Christ and must stand courageously in this world like Judith, praying for the people to convert.

Judith bravely chided her own nation, because it would not trust God's protection, and heroically she delivered it by bravely conquering the enemy. And to combat heroically the evils of

this world, our young ladies must take care that they *look* like a Catholic girl. God was pleased by Judith, because she led a quiet, modest and penitential life, and girls of this age must do the same. A Catholic girl could know her Bible and her religion inside out, but it is her *appearance* which the world sees, and it's her appearance by which the world judges her and other Catholics.

So when a girl goes outside her home, she should examine her appearance. Is it sensual, or careless? Does she by her clothing and appearance give glory to our Father in heaven, or does she want to attract the attention to herself? Nobody who meets her should ever be surprised when he finds out that she is a Catholic. A true

Catholic and Christian girl always dresses modestly, being very careful not to show herself too much, and to draw people's attention to her.

When our girls grow up a little, they will also hear the world speak lots about women's rights, and equality between men and women. But the sad truth is that we live in a world which *despises* women and girls. Movies, magazines, and the Internet are not anymore an entertainment, they are an industry, targeting mostly to make women and girls slaves of the world, instead of being the beauty of their home. A Catholic girl must not and cannot ever try to imitate the so-called stars she might see on TV. Instead, she should always, when thinking how to look and dress, remember the old saying: "If it's not for sale, don't advertise it!"[79] A Catholic girl can never put either her body or her soul up for sale, because the only people who are willing to buy are men of the world, like Holofernes. He would not have listened to anything about the true and just God if Judith had not decorated her body and forced him to listen. And what a miserable end he had. In his life, he was, like modern movie stars and singers, treated almost like a god by his soldiers. But one morning his servant, pa-nicking, shouted to his soldiers: "One Hebrew woman hath made confusion in the house of King Nabuchodonosor: for behold Holofernes lieth upon the ground, and his head is not upon him."[80]

Our heroine Judith was willing to sacrifice herself for her countrymen, out of love for God and His Holy Law. She is a true star, because she was truly to her nation, what the Star of the Sea, the Blessed Virgin Mary, is for the whole of mankind. "Be mindful, O Virgin Mother of God, when thou standest in the sight of the Lord, to speak good things for us, and to turn away His anger from us."[81] Mankind should recommend itself to Our Lady's protection, as the people of Bethulia recommended themselves to the intercession of Judith. Unfortunately, most people neglect to do that, so therefore our Catholic girls should even more recommend themself to heroes and heroines of God, the Saints. Then they, on account of their prayers, will have great power with God. Each day may our girls direct all their doings for the greater glory of God, for this is a great way to chop off the head of pride and obtain heroic virtue in the sight of God.

Chapter 8

Susanna

Susanna sighed, and said: Perplexities are to me on every side: for if I shall do this, it is death to me: and if I do it not, I shall not escape your hands. But it is better for me without the act to fall into your hands, than to sin in the sight of our Lord.

- Daniel 13:22-23

What the citizens of Bethulia had feared, came true less than twenty years after the death of their heroine Judith: Jerusalem fell to foreign troops for the first time in 597 BC. King Joachin had to plead for mercy, and Nabuchodonosor II, king of Babylon, took away the treasures of the Temple and the court of the king. And Nabuchodonosor also transported the court and all the important men into captivity, nearly ten thousand people, leaving behind nothing except the poorest of the people. He also appointed Joachin's uncle Sedecias as his puppet-king.[82]

The history of Susanna took place during this first exile of the Jews in Babylon.* King Nabuchodonosor had made Babylon the capital of his great kingdom, which he decorated with

---

* The history of Susanna is read on the Saturday of the Third week in Lent, and it is the longest epistle of the entire year. It was assigned to that day, because the stational church for that day is that of St. Susanna. The Ambrosian Liturgy beautifully compares Susanna's distress to the Passion of Our Lord. It's read on Holy Thursday, of which it is the first reading, and is followed by a Psalm: "Unjust witnesses rising up, asked me things that I knew not. They repaid me evil things for good." (Ps. 34:11-12) The second reading is from Wisdom 2:12-25, beginning: "In those days the wicked said to each other: Let us there-fore circumvent the just, because he is unprofitable to us, and he is contrary to our works, and reproachfully objecteth unto us the sins of the law, and defameth in us the sins of our discipline." The Gospel that follows immediately after is Matt. 26:14-16, and tells of the be-trayal of Judas, who sells our Lord for thirty pieces of silver. *DiPippo 2011.*

large gardens. These were called the Hanging Gardens of Babylon, one of the Seven Wonders of the Ancient World. Nabuchodonosor, however, during this first exile, allowed the Jews to govern themselves and live according to their own laws. This governing body of judges in Babylon was held in the house of a man named Joakim.

Joakim had a very beautiful wife named *Susanna*. She was not only beautiful, but also pious and God-fearing. Her parents had been very religious, and had raised her according to the Law of Moses. Joakim was a very rich man whose house was located near the gardens. His house was frequented by two old men, who were appointed judges for that year to rule the People of God. But these two judges were very wicked.[83]

Susanna was in the habit of going at noon-time into her husband's garden for a walk with her maids. During these walks the two judges took a liking to her, and started to spy on her. They both fell madly in love with Susanna, and every day spied on her when she was walking in the garden. They started to wait for an opportunity, when Susanna might go to the garden alone. And one day, during the hot season, she dismissed her maids to get her some oils, so that she could take a bath. And not knowing that the two judges were also in the garden, Susanna told the maids to shut the gates so that she could bathe in private.[84]

After the maids had gone, the two judges saw their opportunity. They ran to Susanna, said they were in love with her, and entreated her to commit sin with them. And to further add to their wickedness, they said that if she would not consent, they would lie to everybody, saying that she had been in the garden with a young man, and that this was the reason she had dismissed her maids.[85]

Susanna was distressed in an impossible situation. She sighed and said: "Perplexities are to me on every side: for if I shall do this, it is death to me: and if I do it not, I shall not escape your hands. But it is better for me without the act to fall into your hands, than to sin in the sight of our Lord." Then she started to cry out with a loud voice, and the two judges also star-ted to yell against her. One of them ran to the door of the garden and opened it, and in came the servants of Joakim's house, who had arrived to check what was going on in the garden.[86]

The two judges, according to their threat,

threw the accusation of adultery against Susanna, to the great distress and shame of her household. On the following morning the two wicked judges went to Joakim's house and demanded that Susanna be put to death for adultery. Susanna was escorted in with her parents, her children, and other relatives. To further her humiliation and torture, the judges ordered her to be uncovered, to see her beauty one last time before she faced certain death. In the midst of her misery, Susanna looked up to heaven and prayed to God to deliver her.[87]

The judges started their evil accusation, saying they had spotted Susanna alone with a young man, while they were walking in the garden. They claimed he had escaped before they could seize him. The people believed the lies of the judges, and they, her own persecutors, condemned Susanna to death. She was to be stoned, as it was the case with adulteresses. And Susanna again prayed to God to rescue her from this evil and false accusation. And God heard her prayer. When she was being led to death, God inspired a boy named Daniel, who was then about twelve years old, to stand up and shout: "I

am clean from the blood of this woman." All heads turned to Daniel, who stood up in the middle of them, and claimed that the two judges had given false testimony against Susanna.[88]

Daniel told the people to separate the judges, and he would interrogate them. He then asked the first one, under which tree he had seen Susanna and the young man talking together. The first judge answered that it had happened under a mastic tree. After him, Daniel asked the second judge the same question and he answered: under a prune tree. After hearing this, all the people did to the judges according to the Law of Moses. They put to death the guilty judges and spared the life of innocent Susanna. Her reputation was restored among her family and the people, and from now on everybody knew how great a prophet Daniel was.[89]

Susanna is yet another great heroine of faith to all Catholic girls. In her distress, she was in danger of death on both sides. But she did not even hesitate in her choice. Being left to the hands of the judges would mean certain death, but committing the sin they proposed would mean the death of her soul.

It is also worthy to point out how care-fully Susanna guarded her chastity. First, she did not go out strolling alone, but had her maids as her companions. Then she guarded her modesty very carefully, by sending them away and telling them to shut the gates of the garden that she might bathe in private. She was the very heroine of virtue, who preferred to die rather than sin. Her example shows all Catholic youth how they should act when tempted to sin against holy purity. Susanna called loudly for help to drive the two wicked tempters.

Susanna is also to be remembered in the modern world of instant worldwide communication and social media. One American teacher showed recently very strikingly how dangerous it is to be imprudent in one's actions on the Internet. A sixth-grade teacher, Melissa Bour, in Tulsa, Oklahoma, received a friend request on Facebook at the end of 2014 from one

of her students. She didn't accept the girl's request, but a quick browse through the girl's friends list revealed the names of dozens of kids from her classroom. Many of the students' Facebook pages were completely public, and there Ms. Bour saw indecent gestures, students dressed inappropriately, and extremely foul language. So to make a point, she wrote on a piece of paper in all caps:

> Dear Facebook: My 12-year-old students think it is "no big deal" that they are posting pictures of themselves ... Please help me ... [show them] how quickly their images can get around.

She put a picture of the letter on her Facebook page and asked people to share it. In hours it was shared 108,000 times across dozens of states and four countries. She deleted it after eight hours, but it continued to circulate. As she explained the results of her experiment in class, the students' eyes got bigger and bigger. It scared a few of them into deleting their pages completely. Others removed the inappropriate posts and utilized privacy settings to manage their pages.[90]

In the same way, Catholics should detest all sins of impurity and immodesty much more than the students were horrified at their lack of privacy online. And as much as Catholics abhor the impurity of the two judges, they should love Susanna for her beautiful and honorable virtues. Her body was beautiful, but her soul was a thousand times more so. She was chaste and faithful, because she feared God. She dreaded sin as the greatest of all evils, and choose rather to be publicly calumniated before men and her own family, and to lose her life, than to commit a mortal sin against chastity. The very name Susanna means "a lily", and she has been praised and honored for centuries and millennia as a model of holy fear, fidelity and chastity. We can apply to her the words of the Sacred

Scripture: "As the lily among the thorns, so is my love among the daughters."[91]

The heroic fortitude of Susanna is a great example to every Catholic girl to help her resist temptations against purity, or trying to show herself too much in the eyes of the world. Internet and social media have put the Catholic children under attack even in their homes, and it is the duty of their parents to prevent them to use them, except under specific parental supervision. Neither flattery nor threats should ever be allowed to lead a Catholic girl to sin, but fortified by the prayers of the Church and intercession of her mother in Heaven, the most pure Blessed Virgin Mary, she abandons firmly any impure thought or dishonorable desire.

Chapter 9

Esther

And when Assuerus had lifted up his face, and with
burning eyes had shewed the fury of his breast, Esther
fell down, and her colour being changed into paleness,
she rested her weary head upon her handmaid. And God
turned the King's spirit into mildness, and in haste and
fearing he lept out of the throne, and holding her up in
his arms, till he came to herself, spake her fair.

- Esther 15:10-11

More than any other Old Testament woman saint, Queen Esther is an example of the strength that comes from prayer and fasting. Doing penance, which the Church commands during the great season of Lent, should not be practised in preparing for Easter only, but during one's whole life, in proportion to one's state of life and to the distress or request at hand.

Those Jews, whom King Nabuchodonosor had left in Jerusalem, revolted again in 586 BC, so he returned with a still greater army in 588 BC, and the whole city was given up to fire and destruction. Thousands were killed, and the streets literally ran with blood. The city was sacked, the Temple destroyed, the houses burnt, and the walls overthrown. Now all the people who escaped the massacre were led into captivity in Babylon.

The captive Jews longed to go back to the land of their fathers and to the city of Jerusalem. This longing of their hearts is beautifully sung in one of the Psalms:

Upon the rivers of Babylon, there we sat and wept: while we remembered Sion. On the willows in the

midst thereof, we hanged up our instruments. Because there they that led us captive, demanded of us words of songs. And they that led us away: Sing ye a hymn to us of the songs of Sion. How shall we sing the song of our Lord in a strange land? If I shall forget thee, O Jerusalem, let my right hand be forgotten. Let my tongue cleave to my jaws, if I do not remember thee: If I shall not set Jerusalem in the beginning of my joy.[92]

But during the captivity, God did not abandon His people. He sent them prophets to preach that He still remembered them, and once again to exhort them to prayer and to do penance. And in the seventieth year of their captivity, in 536 BC, Cyrus, king of Persia, by a divine inspiration, gave the Jews permission to go back to Jerusalem and rebuild the Temple.

But because the government of the kings of Persia was very mild, many Jews chose to remain in Babylon. Many of them, like Daniel had been, were in high favor with the kings of Persia. One of these Jews was named Mardocheus, and he lived in Susan. He was one of the last living Jews who had been carried into the first captivity of Babylon*.[93]

The history of the book of Esther took place during the reign of Persian King Darius I the Great. He ascended to the throne in 522 BC, when Mardocheus would have been about 80 years old. In the book of Esther, Darius is called Assuerus. In the second year of Assuerus' reign, he gave an edict of rebuilding the temple.[94] In that same year, in the midst of the joy among Jews, Mardocheus had a dream, where among big thunders and earth-

---

* see p. 107.

quakes two dragons prepared to fight against each other, and the People of God were crying to their Lord in distress. Then a little fountain grew into a very great river, the sun arose and banished the darkness, the humble were exalted and killed the mighty ones. Mardocheus was certain that the dream was from God and desirous to know what it meant.[95]

On the following year, King Assuerus prepared a great feast for his nobles. On the seventh day, when Assuerus was very drunk from wine, he humiliated Queen Vasthi by ordering her to appear before the banquet like a show-piece. When Vasthi rightly refused, she was banished from the court so that the women of the kingdom would not follow her example and rebel against their husbands' demands. Being now without a queen, Assuerus ordered the most beautiful women of his kingdom to be brought in front of him, so he could choose his favorite to become a new queen.[96]

One of the women brought to Susan was *Esther*, the niece of Mardocheus, whom he had adopted after the death of her parents. The King liked Esther more than anyone else, and without knowing that she was a Jew, crowned her as the new Queen.[97]

Some years later, Assuerus appointed a Macedonian man named Aman as his Grand-Vizier, which was the highest in the kingdom after the king. Aman demanded that everyone show him divine adoration, of which Mardocheus refused. This made Aman very angry, and in his fury he decided to exterminate the whole Jewish nation. Aman caused Assuerus to believe that the Jews were treating the king's laws with contempt and observing strange rituals. And because of his lies, Assuerus gave

his permission for the extermination. All Jews, both young and old, as well as little children and women, were to be killed. The day was set, and directions for the massacre were sent to all the provinces, and the Jews in Susan were in terror.[98]

When Mardocheus heard of the coming assault against his nation, he rent his garments, put on sackcloth and placed ashes on his head. He led the lamentation in the city, and people followed his example. When Esther heard of the coming massacre, Mardocheus exhorted her to intercede for her people to the King. She agreed and wrote to him: "Go, and gather together all the Jews, whom thou shalt find in Susan, and pray ye for me. Eat ye not, and drink not in three days, and three nights: and I with my handmaids in like manner will fast, and then will I go in to the King; doing against the law, not called, and delivering myself to death and to peril." Mardocheus did what Esther asked.[99]

Esther was very afraid of seeing the King. As she had written, she took off her royal garments, put on mourning clothes, put ashes on her head and fasted, and prayed:

My Lord, which only art our King, help me solitary woman, and which have no other helper before thee. We have sinned in thy sight, and therefore thou hast delivered us into the hands of our enemies: For we have worshipped their gods. Deliver not O Lord thy scepter to them that are not, lest they laugh at our ruin: but turn their counsel upon them, and destroy him, that hath begun to do cruelly against us. Give me speech well framed in my mouth, in the presence of the lion, and turn his heart into the hatred of our enemy, that both himself may perish, and the rest that consent unto him. And that thy handmaid did never rejoice, since I was transported hither unto

this day, but in thee O Lord the God of Abraham. O God strong above all, hear the voice of them, that have no other hope, and deliver us from the hand of the wicked, and deliver me from my fear.[100]

On the third day Esther removed her penitential attire and put on her fancy royal robes. After asking help from God Almighty, she took her two maids with her, hid her anguish and fear, and presented herself in front of Assuerus. The king was very angry at her for coming uninvited, and looked so terrifying that Esther fainted of fear. Seeing this, Assuerus had a change of heart. By God's power he forgot his fury, and leaped from his throne to Esther. He held her in his arms until she came to her senses, and was assured that she would not die, for the queen has always access to her king. Assuerus promised her that he would give her whatever she would ask, even half of his kingdom, if it pleased her. Esther then said that she would make her request in a feast she had arranged and asked that the king would invite Aman to be there as well. So Aman was invited to the feast. And when he was joyfully returning from the palace, he saw Mardocheus sitting before the gate. He became furious that this old man not only did not adore him, but did not even move from the place he was sitting. His wife Zares convinced him to prepare high gallows, and talk the king over to condemn Mardocheus to be hanged.[101]

King Assuerus could not sleep that night, wondering what Esther might ask. He commanded the chronicles of the past to be brought to him, and found out that Mardocheus had previously exposed the treason of two of Assuerus' ministers who had conspired the assassination of the king. When he heard that Mardocheus had received no reward for exposing the treason, he called in Aman, and asked, what should be done to a man, whom the king wishes to honor? Aman, thinking that the king meant him, answered that that man should be clothed in the robes of the king, the royal crown put on his head; and he should be paraded through the streets of the city. And Assuerus told him to get Mardocheus, and do to him everything Aman had said. The fall of Aman came during the feast of Esther, when she revealed she was a Jew, and that Aman was conspiring to destroy all the Jews of Assuerus' kingdom. It was also revealed, that Aman was preparing to hang Mardocheus, and in his fury the king ordered that Aman must be hanged on the same gallows he had prepared for Mardocheus.[102]

On the same day, when all Jews were designed to be murdered, a new edict of the king was issued, exposing the schemes of Aman, which said:

> But we have found the Jews, which were by that most wicked of men appointed to be slain, in no fault at all, but contrariwise using just laws, and the children of the highest and the greatest, and always loving God, by whose benefit the Kingdom was given both to our fathers and to us, and is kept unto this day. Wherefore know ye those letters, which he

directed in our name, to be of none effect. For the which heinous fact, before the gates of this city, that is of Susan, both himself that devised it, and all his kindred hang on gibbets: not we, but God repaying him that which he hath deserved. But this edict, which we now send, let it be set forth in all cities, that it be lawful for the Jews to use their own laws. Whom you must help, that those which had prepared themselves to their slaughter, they may kill, the thirteenth day of the twelfth month, which is called Adar. For God omnipotent hath turned this day of sadness and mourning into joy to them. Wherefore count you also this day among other festival days, and celebrate it with all joy, that hereafter also it may be known, that all, which faithfully obey the Persians, receive worthy reward for their fidelity: and they that lie in wait against their Kingdom, perish for their wicked fact.[103]

Following the command of the king, the Jews put to death their enemies, who had first pre-pared to kill them. Esther asked the king that the ten sons of Aman also be put to death for treason, and it was done. And as the king had commanded, the day of the Jews' deliverance from slaughter was set as a feast-day, and it is still celebrated by them as the feast of Purim. Mardocheus then under-stood the dream in which he had seen Esther depicted as the little fountain which grew into a river, and that the two dragons were him-self and Aman, and that God had heard the distress of His people, and had had mercy on them.[104]

Queen Esther, in her thrilling history, is in a special way an example of penance. In the hour of the desperate need of her nation, she had recourse to prayer and fasting. Besides using every allowed human means of help, Esther saw prayer and fasting as pleasing to God, and that these would obtain help and salvation from Him. In the same way, when our Lord's disciples were

wondering why they couldn't cast out demons, He answered: "This kind can go out by nothing, but by prayer and fasting."[105]

All of her life Esther had remained humble and obedient to God, even after being raised to be the queen. This confidence in God made it possible for her to risk her own life to save her people. She knew that her passionate king would be in a violent rage when she would appear unsummoned, but she prayed, and hoped that God would soften his heart. And she pre-pared to meet him by prayer and fasting, and with these deeds and with confidence she obtained the deliverance of her people – the People of God – from mass slaughter. She also asked her uncle and her own nation to pray for her, in preparation for this dangerous meeting. She is a type and model for every Catholic girl to have full confidence in the mercy and help of God Almighty, and at the same time, to practice penance and acts of contrition for her own sins and those of her family and country.

Chapter 10
Mother of the Seven Machabees

But the mother above measure marvelous, and worthy of good men's memory, which beholding her seven sons perishing in one day's space, bore it with a good heart, for the hope that she had in God.

- 2 Mach. 7:20

Under the Persians, the Jews lived in peace. The Persian rule ended in 329 BC, when Alexander the Great took possession of Judea and Jerusalem. Alexander was favorable to the Jews and allowed them religious freedom. He died in 323 BC and his son and successor Alexander IV was murdered in 309 BC. After this the Jews lived for a hundred years under the Egyptian rule of the Ptolemaic Dynasty in very free conditions. But this came to an end in the year 200 BC, when Judea was conquered by the kings of Syria, who headed the Hellenistic Seleucid Empire. This state had been formed from the lands of Alexander the Great and got its name from its rulers, the Seleucid dynasty. It became the center of the Hellenistic culture and religion, and also received many immigrants from Greece.

The rulers of this empire were referred to as the kings of Syria. And the worst of the Syrian kings was Antiochus IV Epiphanes, whose father had conquered Judea. The king sold the high-priesthood to his supporter Menelaus, to make sure the government of the Jews was in favorable hands.[106] In the year 169 BC, he attacked

Jerusalem and killed 40,000 inhabitants. He also profaned the Temple, ordered the Holy Books to be torn and burnt, and forbade the observance of the Jewish religion under the penalty of death. Many Jews abandoned the religion of their ancestors be-cause of fear of death and embraced paganism. But many of them refused to obey the tyrant's commands, and chose to die rather than offend God.

Among these martyrs was an old man named Eleazar, who was 90 years old. When he refused to eat swine flesh, they opened his mouth by force to force him to eat. But still he refused, and declared that he would suffer any tortures rather than stain his soul by violation of God's commandment. He was dragged to his place of execution, where he suffered glorious martyrdom.[107]

This holy death of Eleazar was followed by that of seven brothers. The seven Machabee brothers and their mother have the distinction among the Old Testament saints of having their own feast day assigned in the universal calendar. From the first ages of the Church, their feast has been celebrated on August 1. The brothers and their mother, even though their names are not known, are styled Machabees, because the famous resistance leader against the Syrians named Judas Machabeus made his name so famous that all who resisted the persecution of Antiochus were honored by this name.

Antiochus himself commanded that a certain widow with her seven sons should be brought to him. Like Eleazar, the family was also told to eat swine flesh against the Mosaic law. They all told Antiochus to his face that since the divine law forbade such action, they would not obey his command. So Antiochus immediately had them scourged with whips.[108]

The cruel king ordered the six elder brothers to be put to death one by one in the most horrible ways, but all of them stayed firm and confirmed each other in Faith. They did not care about pain and death, because they suffered all for God. And their mother, whom the Bible calls "above measure marvelous", who had to see her sons suffer and put to death, bore all this bravely, because she also hoped in God, and said to them:

> I know not how you appeared in my womb: for neither did I give you spirit and soul and life, and the members of every one I myself framed not. But indeed the Creator of the world, that hath formed the nativity of man, and that invented the origin of all, and He will restore again with mercy unto you spirit and life, as now you despise yourselves for His laws.[109]

The king and his courtiers were amazed at the constancy of these young men. Finally, there was only left the seventh, the youngest one. To him,

who was still a child, Antiochus told, that if he
would obey him rather than God, he would avoid
death and become rich and happy. The king
thought that by these promises he would be able
to induce the boy, as he was young and weak, to
apostatize. But seeing that his words had no
effect on the courageous boy, Antiochus called
the mother to advise her son to save his own
life.[110]

And the mother did so. Then, addressing him with their native Jewish language, which the king could not understand, she said with all the tender affection of a mother:

> My son, have pity on me which have borne thee in my womb nine months, and gave thee milk for three years, and nourished thee, and brought thee unto this age. I beseech thee my son, that thou look to heaven and earth, and to all things that are in them: and understand that God of nothing made them and mankind: so shall it come to pass, that thou wilt not fear this tormenter, but being made a worthy partaker with thy brethren, take thou death, that in that mercy I may receive thee again with thy brethren.[111]

Equally bravely, her young son again stood against Antiochus, exclaimed that he would stay faithful to the Law of God, and cursed the king that he would one day be destroyed by God Almighty. Inflamed with rage, Antiochus tortured the boy most cruelly until he finally died. And last of all, the mother herself was put to death.[112]

It is impossible to admire sufficiently the unshaken fortitude of seven brothers, and even more admirable is the heroism of their mother.

She had most to suffer, for in her heart she suffered all the tortures her sons went through. It was both because of her firm faith in God, as well as her faith in His promise about the future Redeemer, who would defeat the sins and schemes of the world. Since they believed in this way in the Incarnation, the Church has given them the proper feast day.

Her example also teaches many valuable lessons to modern day Catholic girls. It tells us never to obey even lawful superiors, when their laws or commands order us to do anything which God has forbidden, or when they forbid anything which God has commanded.

Also her story points out the obligation of parents in the education of their children. Parents should learn from the mother of the Machabee brothers to bring up their children in the fear and love of God, and also to take care of their souls more than anything else, so that they may look to meet them again in eternal life. When the mother of the Machabee brothers saw that her sons were told to break the law of God, she was as much afraid to leave them here on earth, as other mothers would have been of their death. Her faith was victorious over flesh and blood. An extra-Biblical book named the Fourth Book of the Machabees, highly valued by many of the Church Fathers, praises her with these words:

The mother, when two things were set before her: religion, or the saving of her sons for a time, according to the tyrant's promise, rather chose religion, which saveth to eternal life with God. O in what way can I morally portray the affections of parents to their children? which wondrously stamp a similarity, both of mind and form, on that small distinctive character which each possesses, namely, of being a child! as mothers especially sympathise more strongly than fathers in the sufferings of their children. - - For they were both just, and temperate, and brave, and high-minded, and fond of their brothers; and fond of their mother to such a degree that they obeyed her even unto death, by keeping the injunctions of the law. But yet, although there were so many circumstances of affection which drew on a mother to sympathy: in the case of no one of them were the various tortures able to turn astray her principle. But each child separately, and all of them together, the mother actually encouraged to the death for religion's sake. - - O mother of a nation, avenger of the law, champion of religion, and conqueress in a struggle of affections! O thou who wast more noble in endurance than males, more manly than men in patience! For, as the ark of Noah in the universal deluge, bearing in it the entire world, sustained the violent waves: so thou, observer of the law, though overwhelmed on all sides by a deluge of troubles, and hard pressed by violent winds, namely, the tortures of thy sons, — didst nobly sustain the storms for religion's sake.[113]

In this day and age, so many Christians allow their own will or their own passions to triumph over Faith. Often even one word spoken against us disturbs our minds, and we are provoked so easily at the least sign of contradiction. But neither tortures nor death were able to move the courageous soul of this heroic mother. So many mothers of this day meet daily the sorrows which they have drawn upon themselves by allowing their children to fall through their own bad example or neglect. All Catholic mothers and girls desiring to become mothers should learn from this heroine to raise their children to perfect virtue of Holy Catholic Faith. The little souls have been charged to their care by God Himself and in the mother of the Machabees they see the lasting and living sermon how a mother like her can count as many saints in her family as she is blessed with children.

Extra Chapter
Respha

And Respha the daughter of Aia taking a hair cloth, spread it under her upon the rock from the beginning of harvest, till water dropped upon the bones of the sons of Saul from heaven: and she suffered not the birds to tear them by day, nor the beasts by night.

- 2 Kings 21:10

In the Mass of the anniversary of death for a deceased Catholic, the epistle contains a piece from the second book of Machabees:

> In those days, the most valiant man Judas, making a gathering, sent twelve thousand dracmas of silver to Jerusalem for sacrifice to be offered for sin, well and religiously thinking of the resurrection. For unless he hoped that they that were slain should rise again, it would be superfluous and vain to pray for the dead. And because he considered that they, which had taken their sleep with godliness, had very good grace laid up for them. It is therefore a holy, and healthful cogitation to pray for the dead, that they may be loosed from sins.[114]

The Machabees believed that those who fell were not eternally lost in hell, because they had fought and died in God's honor. But they believed that they had to make satisfaction for the venial sins of their dead. It is a "holy and healthful" thought to pray for the dead, because it proceeds from a living Faith, and also because by these prayers we help both the dead and ourselves.

In the twenty-first chapter of the Second Book of Kings, there is told for us a beautiful story of a mother who is devoted to her dead sons. She is not really a heroine of Faith, but she

showed to every Catholic an exemplary devotion
to the dead, as well as a mother's devotion to her
children and grandchildren.

When Saul had ruled as the king of Israel,
he had oppressed a tribe called the Gabaonites
very unjustly. So they appealed to the new king
David for revenge, demanding that all

descendants of Saul be put to death. And so it was decreed. Saul's two sons and his five grandsons were crucified on a hill.

Then *Respha*, who was the mother and grandmother of these final remnant members of the former king, took her stand on this hill. She watched the bodies of her crucified sons and grandsons. During the days that followed, Respha kept away big vultures that dropped out of the heavens to eat the corpses. During the night she drove off the wild animals, the jackals and hyenas, which had come to the hill to devour the bodies.

The days passed into weeks, and "from the beginning of harvest, till water dropped upon them from heaven," that is, until the rain finally poured down and ended the drought, this devoted mother guarded the bodies of her children.

At last, when the rain came, and King David saw that God's anger against Saul's sin was appeased, he was also told of Respha's devoted vigils. David went and took the bones of the sons and grandsons of Saul, and buried them together with those of Saul.

This mother was concerned with the dead bodies of her children. How much more concerned, then, should a Catholic girl be about the souls of her own family, and in the future, the souls of her children! Even when she is still young, more than any material thing in this world, she needs to think about her own soul. Like Respha, so also Our Lady, whom St. Bonaventure, Doctor of the Church, calls "the Champion of the dying", will be her help in the terrifying hour of departure from this world. And Our Lady has promised to all her devout children to come to them in death as their Queen and their Mother, to give them consolation and hope. In all the days of her life, a Catholic girl should keep in her mind also her death, and the departure of her own dear family members and friends. Mary is invoked on a daily basis many times to "pray for us sinners, now and at the hour of our death." When this prayer is recited as often as possible during her life, a Catholic girl has the assurance of being carried to the Promised Land of Chanaan, her heavenly homeland, when her own hour comes.

So over the hills of Judah,
Along by the vine-rows green,
With Esther asleep on her bosom,
And Rachel her brothers between.

- Julia Gill, *Christ and the Little Ones*.[115]

Credits of illustrations:

Cover: Bernabé de Ayala (1625-1689): "Jael"

p. 14: Julius von Carolsfeld (1794-1872): "Adam and Eve Cover in Shame Before their Judge"

p. 19: Anna Lea Merritt (1844–1930): "Eve in the Garden of Eden"

p. 21: Abraham Bloemaert (1566–1651): "Adam and Eve Grieve over Abel" (Phillip Medhurst, Wikimedia Commons)

p. 23: Caravaggio (1571-1610): "Madonna and Child with St. Anne (Dei Palafrenieri)"

p. 27: Johann Wilhelm Schirmer (1807-1863): "An Angel Rescues Hagar"

p. 30: Peter Paul Rubens (1577–1640): "Hagar Leaves the House of Abraham"

p. 34: Gheorghe Tattarescu (1818-1894): "Agar în the Desert"

p. 35: Charles Henry Granger (1812-1893): "Angel Speaks to Hagar"

p. 37: Giuseppe Bottani (1717–1784): "Hagar and the Angel"

p. 44: Frederick Richard Pickersgill (1820–1900): "Rahab Helping the Two Israelite Spies" (1897)

p. 47: Gustave Doré (1832–1883): "Joshua Spares Rahab"

p. 48: Cecrope Barilli (1839-1911): "Young Roman Girl with a Bunch of Flowers"

p. 53: Carlo Maratta (1625–1713): "Jael shows Barak the corpse of Sisera"

p. 57: Pedro Nuñez del Valle (1597-1649): "Jael and Sisera"

p. 58: James Tissot (1836-1902): "Jael Shows to Barak Sisera Lying Dead"

p. 62: William-Adolphe Bouguereau (1825-1905): "The Prayer" (1865)

p. 70: Gustave Doré (1832–1883): "La fille de Jephté et ses compagnes"

p. 77: Chauncey Ives (1810–1894): "Jephthah's Daughter" in the Atlanta High Museum of Art

p. 81: Hugues Merle (1823–1881): "Ruth in the Fields" (1876)

p. 84: Julius Hübner (1806–1882): "Ruth and Naomi" (1831)

p. 86: Joseph Anton Koch (1768-1839): "Landscape with Ruth and Boaz"

p. 95: Sebastiano del Piombo (1485-1547): "Judith and Holofernes" (1525)

p. 97: Adolphe François Pannemaker (1822-1900): "Judith" (Alamy Stock Photo)

p. 99: Luca Giordano (1634–1705): "Judith Displaying the Head of Holofernes"

p. 108: Ferdinand Knab (1834-1902): "The Hanging Gardens of Babylon" (1886)

p. 110: Peter Lely (1618–1680): "Susanna and the Elders"

p. 112: Philip James de Loutherbourg (1740-1812): "Daniel Convicting the Elders" (Phillip Medhurst, Wikimedia Commons)

p. 119: Franz Caucig (1755–1828): "Esther before Ahasuerus" (1815)

p. 124: Ernest Normand (1857–1923): "Vashti Deposed" (1890)

p. 128: Guercino (1591–1666): "Esther Before Ahasuerus"

p. 131: Gustave Doré (1832–1883): "Esther Accuses Haman"

p. 138: Philip James de Loutherbourg (1740-1812): "Sacrilege of Antiochus"

p. 141: Gustave Doré (1832–1883): "The Courage of a Mother"

p. 150: Gustave Doré (1832–1883): "Rizpah protecting the corpses of her sons"

Sources:

Articles:

DiPippo, Gregory
2011   The Story of Susanna in the Liturgy of Lent. – < http://www.newliturgicalmovement.org/2011/04/story-of-susanna-in-liturgy-of-lent.html >.

Jung, Alyssa
2015   A Lesson Goes Viral. – Reader's Digest. May 2015. Harlan, IA.

Pitluk, Adam
2015   Story of a Life. – < http://magazines.aa.com/content/story-life >. American Way. June 2015.

Books:

ACCOS
2000   Ancient Christian Commentary on Scripture. Vol. New
       Testament XI. Edited by Gerald Bray. Downers Grove,
       IL: InterVarsity Press.
2001   Ancient Christian Commentary on Scripture. Vol. Old
       Testament I. Edited by Andrew Louth. Downers Grove,
       IL: InterVarsity Press.
2002   Ancient Christian Commentary on Scripture. Vol. Old
       Testament II. Edited by Mark Sheridan. Downers Grove,
       IL: InterVarsity Press.
2005   Ancient Christian Commentary on Scripture. Vol. Old
       Testament IV. Edited by John R. Franke. Downers Gro-
       ve, IL: InterVarsity Press.

Alphonsus Liguori, St.
1852   The Glories of Mary. New York, NY: Edward Dunigan
       and Brothers.

Borthwick, J. Douglas (ed.)
1866   The Harp of Canaan; or Selections from the Poets on
       Bible Historical Incidents. Montreal: Richard Wor-
       thington.

Cotton, Henry (ed.)
1832   The Five Books of Maccabees in English. Oxford Uni-
       versity Press.

Currier, Charles Warren
1894   History of Religious Orders. New York, NY: Murphy &
       McCarthy.

Ghéon, Henri
2011   The Truth About Thérèse. An Unflinching Look at
       Lisieux, the Little Flower, and the Little Way. Man-
       chester, NH: Sophia Institute Press.

Kelley, Francis C.
1922 Dominus Vobiscum. A Book of Letters. Chicago, IL: Matre & Company.

Knecht, Frederick Justus
1910 A Practical Commentary on Holy Scripture for the Use of Those Who Teach Bible History. B. Herder.

Mary of Agreda
1872 Divine Life of the Most Holy Virgin Mary; being an abridgment of the Mystical City of God. Philadelphia, PA: Peter F. Cunningham.

McDonald, Stacy
2011 Raising Maidens of Virtue. A Study of Feminine Loveliness for Mothers and Daughters. Revised & Expanded Edition. Sand Springs, OK: Grace & Truth Books.

O'Sullivan, Paul
1993 Saint Philomena the Wonder-Worker. Rockford, IL: TAN Books and Publishers.

Roman Breviary
1908 The Roman Breviary. Vol. I. Winter. Translated out of Latin into English by John, Marquess of Bute. Edinburgh: William Blackwood and Sons.

Talmud
1886 The Talmud of Jerusalem. Vol. I. Berakhoth. Translated for the first time by Dr. Moses Schwab. London: Williams and Norgate.

Endnotes:

[1] Gen. 2:20-21.
[2] ACCOS 2001, 64. Tertullian in Against Marcion.
[3] Gen. 2:9.
[4] Gen. 2:17. All quotations from the Holy Scripture used in this book are from the original Douay-Rheims Bible, published in Reims, France, in 1582 (New Testament), and in Douai, France, in 1609-1610 (Old Testament).
[5] Gen. 3:4-5.
[6] Gen. 3:12.
[7] Gen. 3:13.
[8] ACCOS 2001, 87. Dorotheus of Gaza, Spiritual Instruction.
[9] Gen. 3:16.
[10] Gen. 3:21-24.
[11] Watson 1871, 9-10.
[12] Eph. 2:3.
[13] Gen. 3:19.
[14] Gen. 4:7.
[15] Gen. 4:9.
[16] Gen. 4:16.
[17] Life of Adam and Eve.
[18] Gen. 3:15.
[19] Roman Breviary 1908, 268.
[20] Gen. 12:1-5.
[21] Gen. 16:1-9.
[22] Gen. 16: 10-11.
[23] Gen. 16:13-15.
[24] Gen. 17:5-8.
[25] ACCOS 2002, 94. St. Ephrem the Syrian.
[26] Gen. 21:9-13.
[27] Gen. 21: 14-18.
[28] Gen. 21:19-21.
[29] ACCOS 2002, 98. St. John Chrysostom.
[30] Alphonsus Liguori 1852, 258. (Chapter 8).
[31] Josue 2:1-7.
[32] Josue 2:8-13.
[33] Josue 2:9-19.

[34] Josue 6:1-21.
[35] James 2:24-25.
[36] Josue 2:11.
[37] Matt. 1:5.
[38] ACCOS 2000, 33. Severian of Gabala.
[39] Talmud 1886, 50.
[40] Judges 4:1-2.
[41] Judges 4:3-9.
[42] Judges 4:15-17.
[43] Judges 4:18-19.
[44] Judges 4:21.
[45] Judges 4:22-24.
[46] Judges 4:6-7.
[47] Pitluk 2015.
[48] Pitluk 2015.
[49] Ecclesiasticus 22:3-4.
[50] cf. McDonald 2011, 128-129.
[51] Judges 11:30-31.
[52] Judges 11:35.
[53] "Jephthah Keeps His Vow to Jehovah". The Watchtower, 2007, 5/15 pp. 8-10.
[54] Judges 11:31.
[55] Judges 11:39.
[56] Kelley 1922, 150-152.
[57] Mary of Agreda 1872, 71.
[58] Judges 11:36.
[59] Matt. 5:5.
[60] ACCOS 2005, 140. St. Ambrose.
[61] ACCOS 2005, 140. St. Augustine.
[62] O'Sullivan 1993, 87-93.
[63] Currier 1894, 358-359.
[64] Ecclesiasticus 7:40.
[65] Ruth 1:1-2.
[66] Ruth 1:3-9.
[67] Ruth 1:14-15.
[68] Ruth 1:16.
[69] Ruth 2:1-12.
[70] Ruth 3:11.
[71] Ruth 4:11-22.

[72] Ghéon 2011, 20-21.
[73] Judith 7.
[74] Judith 8:1-8.
[75] Judith 8:10-15, 26-27.
[76] Judith 13:7.
[77] Judith 13:8-11.
[78] Judith 15:10.
[79] McDonald 2011, 45.
[80] Judith 14:16.
[81] Offertory of the Mass of Seven Sorrows.
[82] 4 Kings 24:11-17.
[83] Daniel 13:1-6.
[84] Daniel 13:7-18.
[85] Daniel 13:19-21.
[86] Daniel 13:22-26.
[87] Daniel 13:27-35.
[88] Daniel 13:36-50.
[89] Daniel 13:51-64.
[90] Jung 2015.
[91] Cant. 2:2.
[92] Ps. 136:1-6.
[93] Esther 2:5-6; 11:4.
[94] 1 Esdras 4:23-24. There is some dispute, which of the Persian kings Assuerus was. Bishop F.J. Knecht favors the traditional view of him being Xerxes I, who ruled 485-465. But the only one who corresponds to both of the names recorded to him in Sacred Scripture – Darius, Assuerus, and Artaxerxes interchan-geably – and to the age of Mardocheus, is Darius the Great. (cfr. 3 Esdras 4:42-47). This is also the opinion of Fr. Leo Haydock.
[95] Esther 11:5-12.
[96] Esther 1:1-2:4.
[97] Esther 2:5-17.
[98] Esther 3.
[99] Esther 4.
[100] Esther 14.
[101] Esther 5:3-14; 15:4-13.
[102] Esther 6-7.
[103] Esther 16:15-23.
[104] Esther 9-10.

[105] Mark 9:29.
[106] 2 Mach. 4:24-25.
[107] 2 Mach. 6.
[108] 2 Mach. 7:1.
[109] 2 Mach. 7:20-23.
[110] 2 Mach. 24-25.
[111] 2 Mach. 7:27-29.
[112] 2 Mach. 7:30-41.
[113] Cotton 1832, 263-267.
[114] 2 Mach. 12:43-46.
[115] Borthwick 1866, 207.

Made in the USA
Middletown, DE
24 July 2022